Immigrants at Work:
A Look at Migrant Labor

by
Mary Dismas

Editorial Offices: Glenview, Illinois • Parsippany, New Jersey • New York, New York
Sales Offices: Needham, Massachusetts • Duluth, Georgia • Glenview, Illinois
Coppell, Texas • Ontario, California • Mesa, Arizona

Every effort has been made to secure permission and provide appropriate credit for photographic material. The publisher deeply regrets any omission and pledges to correct errors called to its attention in subsequent editions.

Unless otherwise acknowledged, all photographs are the property of Scott Foresman, a division of Pearson Education.

Photo locators denoted as follows: Top (T), Center (C), Bottom (B), Left (L), Right (R), Background (Bkgd)

Opener ©Jim Sugar/Corbis; 1 ©Peter Turnley/Corbis; 3 California Department of Parks and Recreation State Museum Resource Center; 4 Sue Carlson; 6 ©Hulton Archive/ Getty Images; 8 Bettmann/Corbis; 9 Corbis-Bettmann; 10 ©Jim Sugar/Corbis; 12 ©Kevin Fleming/Corbis; 13 ©Dave G. Houser/Corbis; 14 ©Peter Turnley/Corbis; 16 ©Jim Sugar/ Corbis; 18 ©Farrell Grehan/Corbis; 19 ©Najlah Feanny/Corbis; 22 ©Darrell Gulin/Corbis

ISBN: 0-328-13655-7

Copyright © Pearson Education, Inc.

All Rights Reserved. Printed in the United States of America. This publication is protected by Copyright, and permission should be obtained from the publisher prior to any prohibited reproduction, storage in a retrieval system, or transmission in any form by any means, electronic, mechanical, photocopying, recording, or likewise. For information regarding permission(s), write to: Permissions Department, Scott Foresman, 1900 East Lake Avenue, Glenview, Illinois 60025.

8 9 10 V0G1 14 13 12 11 10 09 08

People come to the United States from other countries for many reasons. These Japanese immigrants came to the United States through Angel Island in California.

Who Are Immigrants?

Immigrants are people who come into a new land or nation to live there. For hundreds of years, people have left their friends, relatives, and homelands to live in the United States.

There are many reasons people immigrate. Some of those reasons are listed below. Compare the "push" and "pull" factors. How are they alike? How are they different?

Why do immigrants choose the United States? Many immigrants believe the United States is a place where everyone has more personal freedom—where everyone has **access** to opportunities that will improve their lives.

Why People Immigrate

Push Factors	Pull Factors
• Human rights violations • Economic problems and poverty • Environmental problems and natural disasters	• Expectation of finding work • Expection of joining relatives • Expectation of getting an education • Expectation of living a better life

3

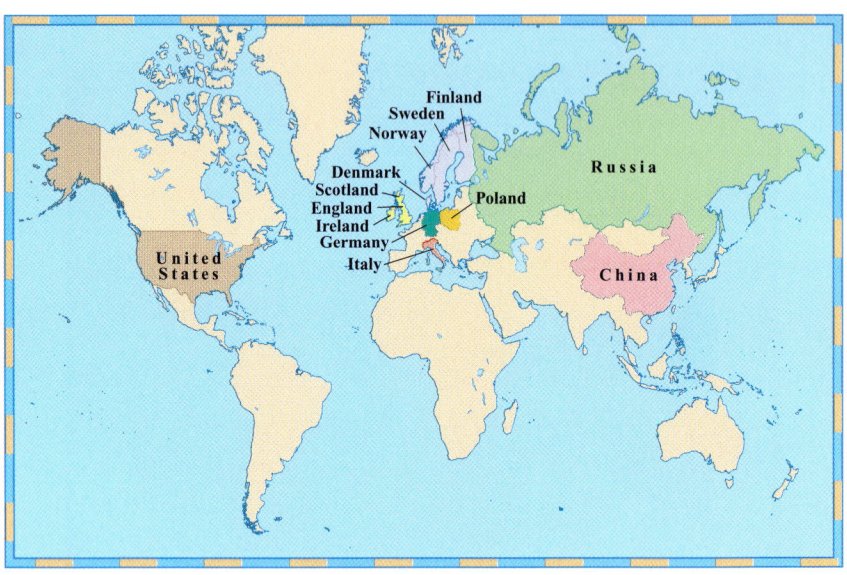

Where Are Immigrants From?

Before the Revolutionary War, most immigrants came from northern European countries such as England, Ireland, and Scotland. From the mid-1800s through the early 1900s, about 25 million people came to the United States from Ireland, Germany, Italy, Poland, Russia, China, Scandinavia, and other countries.

The table below compares the number of people living in New York City and San Francisco, California, in 1870 and 2000. It also shows what percentage of the population was born outside the United States. How did the percentage of foreign-born people living in both cities change from 1870 to 2000?

Year	Total Population	Native Born	Foreign Born	
1870			Number	Percent
New York City	942,292	523,198	419,094	44.5
San Francisco	149,473	75,754	73,719	49.3
2000				
New York City	8,008,278	5,137,246	2,871,032	35.9
San Francisco	776,733	491,192	285,541	36.8

Source: U.S. Bureau of the Census

North America has been a destination point for immigrants since colonial times.

Challenges to Immigrants

Moving to a new country is not an easy thing to do. An immigrant leaves behind a home, relatives and friends, and familiar surroundings and customs. An immigrant may very likely not be fluent in the language of his or her new country. Think about how you would feel if you were not able to understand what people were saying to you. What would you do if you could not make yourself understood by others?

Many immigrants choose to live near other people from their own country because they all speak the same language and practice the same customs. More established immigrants often help newcomers from their homeland find food, clothing, shelter, and jobs.

Some Americans have worried that their jobs would be given to immigrants. Immigrants have at times been treated with hostility and resentment. Some immigrants have been denied the right to become U.S. citizens. Without citizenship, they do not have many rights guaranteed by the U.S. Constitution.

Poverty and discrimination often take their **toll** on many immigrants, and they decide to return to their homelands. Some have become ill and died because of the poor conditions in which they live in their new land. Others have stayed and worked hard to make the United States their new home.

Immigrants in the Nineteenth Century

The first goal of most immigrants in the 1800s was to find a job to support themselves and their families, just as it is today. Some intended to stay in the United States. Others planned to work for a period of time, save money, and then return home. Either way, immigrants needed to find jobs.

Chinese immigrants came to find their fortunes during the California Gold Rush.

Chinese Immigrants

Immigrants came to California from China looking for economic opportunities. Some were also seeking to escape political problems in their homeland. Some hoped to make their fortunes during the Gold Rush. As a matter of fact, some Chinese immigrants referred to California as *Gam Saan,* or "Golden Mountain."

The Chinese made many contributions to the mining industry but were prevented from making their fortunes. California had laws that kept the Chinese from owning land, and they were heavily taxed if they tried to file mining claims.

Despite the **torments** of discrimination, Chinese immigrants continued to arrive in the United States. Some worked to build the railroads. Many had been farmers in their homeland, and so they sought work as farmers. Some became sharecroppers, or tenant farmers, while others became migrant farm workers who traveled from farm to farm harvesting crops as they became ripe.

Many Chinese immigrants were skilled at farming. They were able to turn poor land into fertile farmland, and they knew how to grow specialty crops such as celery. The Chinese played a major role in the growth of the wine industry in California.

Italian Immigrants

In the late 1800s, many Italians came to the United States to escape poverty in their homeland. More than half of those Italian immigrants had been farmers, but they did not want to be farmers in this country. Many Italians planned to stay in the United States only long enough to work and save money, at which time they hoped to return to Italy. The money they saved would allow them to have a better life in their homeland.

Some Italian immigrants found jobs in small businesses. Most, however, worked as unskilled laborers in mines, on the railroad, and in construction. Some who turned to farming in the United States eventually became part of the California wine industry.

Many immigrants arrived in the United States at Ellis Island in New York.

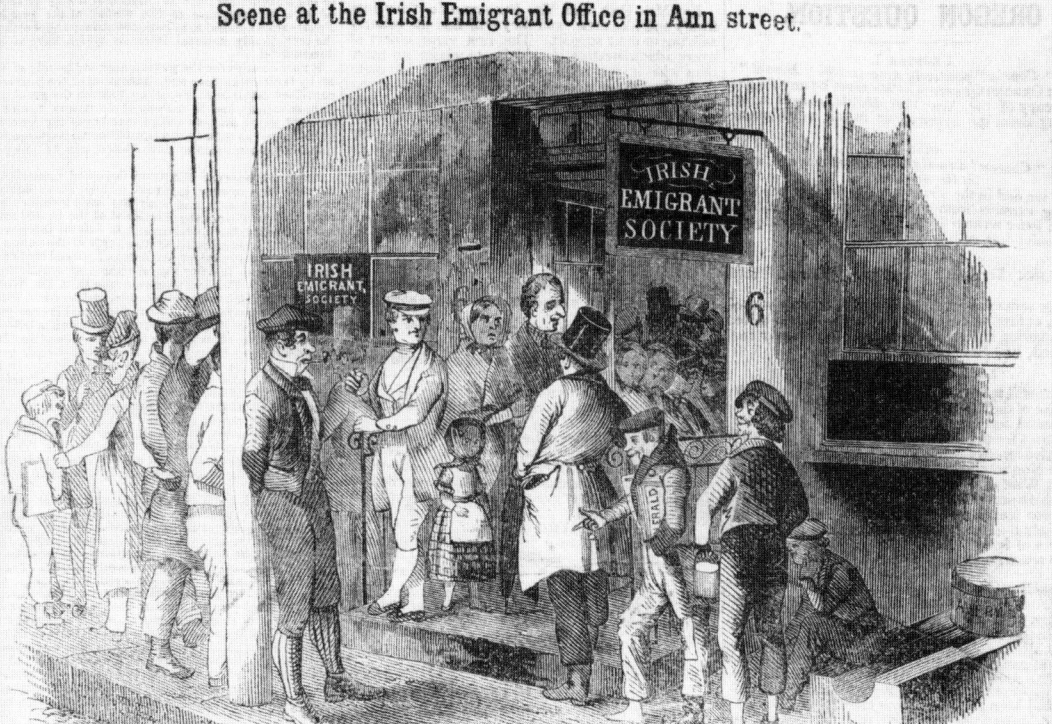

Crowded tenement buildings were unhealthful places to live.

Irish Immigrants

The story of Irish immigrants is somewhat similar to that of the Italians. Many Irish had been farmers in Ireland but were too poor to buy farmland in the United States. They settled in large cities in the Northeast and tried to find work as unskilled laborers.

The low-paying jobs they found forced them to live in overcrowded slum areas. Many people became ill and died from diseases such as tuberculosis and diphtheria.

Irish immigrants had one important advantage—they spoke English. They were still discriminated against, but at least they could communicate with other Americans.

Today's Immigrants

How are conditions different for today's immigrants? They face many of the same challenges as those who came before them. The same "push-pull" factors cause them to leave their homelands. Language barriers still exist, and discrimination and poor treatment make progress toward personal goals more difficult.

Most immigrants in the past ten years have come to the United States from Latin America, the Caribbean, and Asia. The table below shows a portion of the number of immigrants who entered the United States in 2004. Many are educated and able to work in technology or business careers. As in the past, however, some uneducated or unskilled immigrants take jobs as farm workers.

Immigration 2004

Country of Last Residence	Number of Immigrants
Mexico	173,664
India	65,472
Philippines	54,632
China	45,942
Vietnam	30,064
Dominican Republic	30,049
Cuba	15,385
Jamaica	13,565
Haiti	13,502
Japan	8,652

Source: U.S. Citizenship and Immigration Services

Many fruits and vegetables we enjoy are from farms where immigrant laborers work.

America's Migrant Farm Workers

Agriculture in the United States could not exist without farm workers. Without their labor, there would be no food industry. There would be a serious shortage of food. Some migrant workers in the United States are U.S. citizens, but many are immigrants as well.

Farm workers plant, cultivate, and harvest much of our nation's crops. They cultivate and harvest many crops by hand so that Americans can buy fresh, undamaged produce. These same farm workers also make sure crops are shipped to markets or canning factories before they wilt or spoil.

Workers who travel from place to place to find work are called migrant workers.

Each year between one and three million farm workers travel around the country to work on farms during the growing season. Some workers travel with their families. Others live in groups that travel and work under the **authority** of a crew leader.

There are workers who live and work on just one farm. Others travel from place to place. They are called migrant farm workers. Some may stay in the same region or state, but they travel from farm to farm during the planting, growing, and harvesting seasons.

For example, a group of migrant workers might have jobs on a vegetable farm in spring and summer. They might then harvest apples in the fall at an apple orchard. In December, perhaps they'll work on a tree farm cutting down trees.

Some migrant farm workers have permanent homes in Mexico, California, Texas, or Florida. They leave their homes and move to farms all across the United States as their work is needed to plant, cultivate, and harvest crops.

In the past, it was common for farm owners to go out and recruit workers.

Hiring Migrant Farm Workers

Owners of small and large farming operations hire migrant workers because they are a source of cheap and temporary labor. Despite the low wages, a migrant farm worker in the United States can earn about three times the amount of money a worker in Central America can earn doing the same job.

Farm owners don't have to go out looking to recruit their workers. Immigrants often refer friends and family to farm owners who are fair employers. Immigrants who are already employed as migrant farm workers often send word to friends and family in their homelands with a promise of work.

Fast Facts About Earning a Living as a Farm Worker
- In 2002, the average hourly wage for farm workers was $6.84.
- Some farm workers are not paid by the hour. They earn a set price for every container they fill.
- In 2002, half of all farm workers earned less than $7,500.
- In 2002, half of all farm worker families earned less than $10,000.
- Farm workers do not earn any money when there is bad weather, when they are sick, or during the time it takes them to travel from job to job.
- Most farm workers are not protected by labor laws in the states in which they work.
- Some employers do not report the wages they pay to immigrant farm workers, especially if those workers are not legal immigrants. These workers may be unable to claim rightful benefits such as Social Security. They will not have proof of their past employment.

Sometimes farm workers must work with soil and plants that have been sprayed with pesticides and fertilizers.

Living Conditions and Other Hazards

Imagine traveling hundreds of miles to begin a new job only to find that you have nowhere to live. Farm owners realize that they should provide adequate housing for their farm workers, yet many don't do so because of the expenses involved. Workers may be forced to share a room. In the very worst cases, they may find themselves living in tents, cars, ditches, or fields. In the most serious cases, workers lack clean drinking water, water for bathing, and bathroom facilities.

Farm work is outdoor work, and it must be done in the fields no matter what the weather. Workers may be required to work many long hours in order to harvest a crop on time.

Farming can be a dangerous occupation. Many farm accidents are caused each year by operating heavy machinery. Farm work is physically difficult, as workers must constantly stoop, lift, and carry heavy loads. Workers must also handle plants and soil that have been treated with pesticides and fertilizers. This contact can cause allergic skin reactions and respiratory problems.

The Rights of Migrant Workers

Sometimes employers refused to pay migrant farm workers for their labor. Workers kept silent because they were afraid of losing their jobs. They did not realize that they could speak out against the unfair treatment. They didn't think about joining unions. Unions are groups that fight for the fair treatment of and fair wages for workers.

When farm workers belong to an organized union, they have more power to deal with unfair farm owners. Perhaps you have heard the saying "there is strength in numbers." An organized group has a stronger voice than one person alone.

Some farm owners have been against unions for farm workers. They worry that organized workers would demand higher wages and better living conditions, which would, obviously, affect profits.

Workers join together and carry signs, march, and make speeches in an attempt to get better treatment.

A Worker for the Workers

Cesar Chavez was the son of migrant farm workers. As he grew up, he noticed the ways in which farm owners took advantage of workers, and he decided to do something about it. He became an advocate for migrant farm workers all across the country. He worked hard to improve the lives and working conditions of farm workers in the United States.

In 1948, Chavez began to teach Mexican farm workers to read and write English. He did this because adult immigrants did not always have access to schools. Once they learned to read and write English, they were able to take the test required to become American citizens. They were also able to read and understand laws written in English.

Cesar Chavez was a union organizer who worked on behalf of poor farm workers.

In the 1960s, Chavez organized farm workers into a union called the United Farm Workers. This union demanded better pay and better working conditions for its members. California's grape growers ignored the union's demands, and the farm workers went on strike. The grapes went unpicked.

Then the union called for a **boycott.** Consumers were asked not to buy grapes grown in the United States until grape growers improved working conditions for their farm workers. Many Americans joined the boycott. It was very successful. The boycott was lifted in 1970 after grape growers signed contracts giving farm workers much-needed benefits.

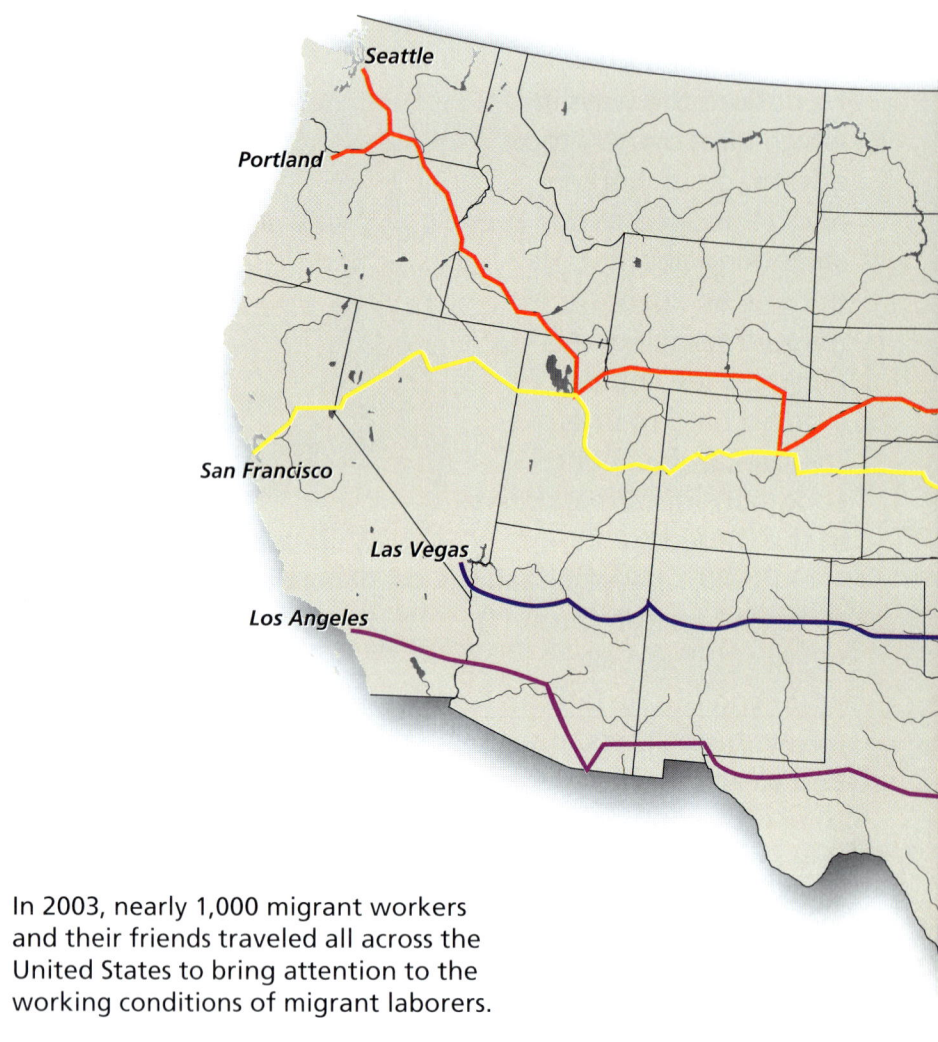

In 2003, nearly 1,000 migrant workers and their friends traveled all across the United States to bring attention to the working conditions of migrant laborers.

Organizing for Action

When organized migrant farm workers see the need, they can gather in public to call attention to their situation. Marches and demonstrations can put pressure on farm owners to treat their workers fairly.

Sometimes, as in the grape boycott, the public will stop buying a farm's products when they are informed

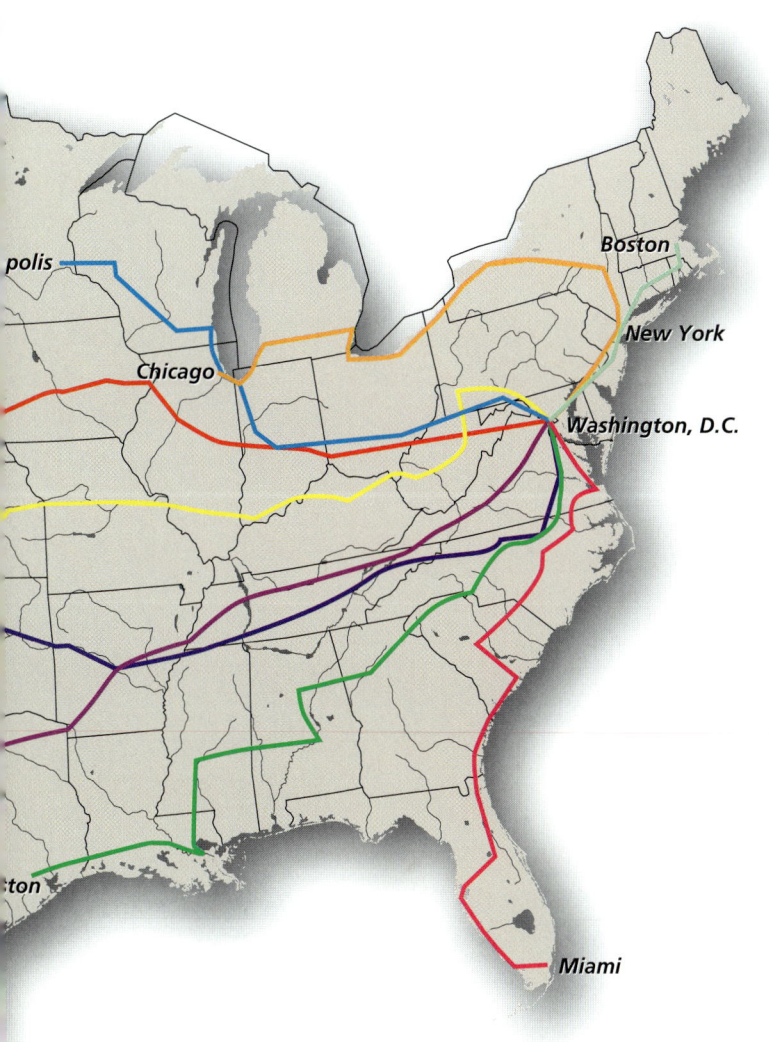

about the poor working conditions and the unfair treatment of workers. By boycotting the farm's products, people show their support for the migrant workers' demands. The loss of profit sometimes makes the farm owner listen to the workers' demands.

The Future for Migrant Workers

Migrant farm workers are no longer silent. They can join other farm workers to speak out for improved working conditions, better pay, and equal rights. There are fewer obstacles on the path to a better life for these workers and their families.

It takes many people to work the lush and fertile farmland in the United States. Recent immigrants and others who take jobs as migrant farm workers may not speak English or know local customs. Still, they have the same dreams as you—a good life and a better future.

The next time you eat an ear of corn, munch an apple, or peel an orange, you might give some thought to the people whose hard work brings food to your table.

The rich and beautiful farmland in the United States is worked by many people. Many workers have come to the United States from their homelands. They might not speak English or know local customs. But these immigrant laborers help grow foods that feed people in the United States and around the world.

Glossary

access *n.* the right or ability to have something.

authority *n.* the power to make decisions or give orders.

lush *adj.* growing in abundance.

obstacles *n.* things that stand in the way.

toll *n.* something paid, lost, or suffered.

torments *n.* very painful events.

wilt *v.* to become limp.